THE POWER OF P(

Unlocking the Health Benefits of Resistant
Starch

Tony Steele

Preface

Welcome to "The Power of Potatoes: Unlocking the Health Benefits of Resistant Starch". We'll take an adventurous trip into the wonders of potato and their secret ingredient: resistant starch, as part of this book. This book is intended to provide you with an overall understanding of the power which potatoes have, whether you are a potato lover or want to know more about possible health benefits.

We'll examine the science behind resistance starch, and how it affects a number of different aspects of our health, in this book. We'll look at the connection between potatoes and weight management, we'll probe into the realm of gut health, find out what secrets are kept to sustain energy. And we'll give you real tips on making potatoes a part of your everyday life.

But this is not just a book about science and theory. The story is also about the real life experiences that potatoes bring to people's lives, and their impact on them. We will share success stories and testimonials that will inspire and motivate you on your own journey.

Let's encourage you to look at the information in this book from a new angle before we start our potatofilled adventure. Each person has a special way of functioning and it can't all work out for the same person. Listening to your body, seeking medical advice if necessary and making decisions that correspond with your own health objectives are essential.

Now, my dear reader, let's go on a journey that is filled with excitement. We need to discover the secret of potatoes, become aware of their ability to resist starch and create a world with health and vitality.

Are you ready? Let's begin our exploration of "The Power of Potatoes: Unlocking the Health Benefits of Resistant Starch!"

Table Of Contents

The Power Of Potatoes

Introduction

Welcome to "The Power of Potatoes: Unlocking the Health Benefits of Resistant Starch!" And this book introduces you to a fascinating world of potatoes, and the remarkable health and wellness benefits that they offer. Let us begin by a compelling short story that will illustrate the transformative power of potatoes before we examine scientific and practical aspects.

Short Story: Emily's Remarkable Journey

Emily's weight and energy levels were difficult for her to handle, just like everyone else. She'd tried out a number of diets or exercises, and failed to produce any results. She felt disappointed, and came upon a story of a woman who had turned her life around after adopting the power of potatoes. Intrigued, Emily decided to give it a shot.

Emily inserted potatoes into her diet when she was learning about resistance starch and the remarkable effects of it. She'd been experimenting with different cooking techniques, and enjoyed a wide variety of flavours they were bringing to the table. After a couple of weeks, she'd gained more energy, had lost weight, been able to stomach better, regained her confidence.

Emily was sharing her journey with other people because of her own success, giving rise to curiosity and hope. They set out to invent a potato revolution, experimenting with new recipes and promoting each other's pursuit of healthy living.

Well, you get to take part in this potato adventure. Within this book, we will guide you through the science, practical tips, and delicious recipes that will unlock the incredible power of potatoes. Prepare for a transformation of your health and an embrace of the new, energetic you.

Are you ready? Let's dive into the world of potatoes and uncover the secrets of resistant starch together!

Chapter 1

Understanding Resistant Starch

We will take a look at resistant starch in this chapter, unravel it's special characteristics and find out how that can have positive effects on health and well being. You'll have a solid understanding of what resistant starch is, its various types, and its incredible benefits by the end of this chapter. Let's start this journey with each other and figure out the secret of resistance starch!

The Basics of Starch

Let's start by taking a basic look at the specific characteristics of resistant starch. In our diet, starch constitutes a complex carbohydrate and serves as the primary source of energy. In a number of standard foods such as potatoes, wheat and legumes it is also in high demand. When we consume starch, it undergoes digestion in our bodies, breaking down into glucose molecules that fuel our cells.

Introducing Resistant Starch

Resistant starch, as the name suggests, is a unique form of starch that resists digestion in the small intestine and reaches the large intestine intact. Resistant starch is nearly completely undigested, owing to the fact that it does not break down quickly into glucose. It's because of its unusual chemical structure and resistance to enzymes that we have in our digestion system.

Types of Resistant Starch

There are several types of resistant starch, each of which has its own characteristics and sources. Let's explore the four main types of resistant starch:

1. RS1: Physically inaccessible starch: In the cellular structure of foods like cereal, legumes or seeds, such a type of resistance starch is

physically attached to them. It's resistant to digestion, since our digestive enzymes can't easily get into it.

2. RS2: Resistant granules: RS2 is found in raw or partially cooked foods, For example, a raw potato and green bananas. Due to the special composition of starch, these products contain granules which are resistant to digestion.

3. RS3: Retrograded starch: When certain starchy foods like cooked and cooled potatoes or rice are reheated, their starch undergoes retrogradation. In this way, digestible starch is converted to a resistance form, known as RS3.

4. RS4: Chemically modified starch: RS4 refers to starch that has been chemically modified to resist digestion. In order to improve the properties of texture, stability and other functions, this substance is commonly applied as an additive in processing foods.

The Health Benefits of Resistant Starch

Now that we understand the different types of resistant starch, let's explore the numerous health benefits it offers:

1. Improved Digestive Health: Resistant starch acts as a prebiotic, which means that it is feeding on beneficial bacteria in the gut. These bacteria are fermenting resistance starch, which contains shortchain fatty acids that nourish the cells in your colon and help you to have a good digestion.

2. Enhanced Insulin Sensitivity: The effect of resistant starch has been demonstrated on insulin sensitivity, which is an advantage for individuals with insulin resistance or type 2 diabetes. It helps with the regulation of your blood sugar level and can help prevent you from getting diabetes.

3. Increased Satiety and Weight Management: Resistance starch may make you feel fuller, which might lead to a decrease in calorie consumption because of its special properties. If you include resistant starch in your diet, it can help with weight loss and support good eating habits.

4. Lowered Risk of Chronic Diseases: Resistant starch has been associated with a decrease in the incidence of various chronic diseases, such as colon cancer. The fermentation in the colon produces beneficial substances that protect the colon cells.

Incorporating Resistant Starch into Your Diet

Now that you're aware of the incredible benefits of resistant starch, you may wonder how to incorporate it into your daily diet. Here are a few practical tips to get you started:

1. Embrace Whole Foods: Try to include whole foods rich in resistant starch, for example cooked and cooled potatoes, green bananas, legumes or grains of all kinds.

2. Cook and Cool: You should cook them and allow them to cool before eating, when preparing foods such as potatoes or rice. The resistance content of the starch shall be increased by this process.

3. Experiment with Recipes: Check out creative recipes which include resistant starch foods. You can make potato salad, add Green bananas to smoothies or incorporate legumes in soup and stews.

4. Gradual Changes: In order that your digestive system is adapted, introduce resistant starch in a gradual fashion to the diet. It may cause digestive distress in sudden large increases, so take it slowly.

You have gained complete understanding of resistant starch and the amazing benefits that it provides. You can increase your ability to digest food with resistant starch while increasing insulin sensitivity, managing weight better and reducing the risk for long term conditions such as heart disease or diabetes if you include resistant starchrich foods in your diet. We'll take a deeper look at implementing resistance starch throughout your day to day life with the next chapters of this book. You are going to find delicious recipes, meal plans, successful stories and more!

Chapter 2

The Potato Phenomenon

We'll be exploring the world of potatoes, revealing their historical importance, nutrition and dispelling myths about how they contribute to weight gain during this chapter. You're going to learn a lot more about potatoes at the end of this chapter and understand what they can do for your diet. Then we're going to get down to the phenomenon of potatoes!

A Storied History

There is a long and storied history in potatoes, dating back thousands of years. The potatoes were originally grown in the Andes, a region of South America, and have been cultivated by old civilizations such as Incas. Their adaptability, their nutritional value, and their ability to thrive in a variety of climatic conditions were highly valued. By the time exploration and colonization had taken place, potatoes were spreading around the world to become one of the most widely cultivated crops in the world.

Nutritional Composition

Potatoes aren't all empty carbohydrates, unlike some people think. It is a nutrient rich food which may be able to provide many basic vitamins, minerals and fibres. We're going to look into the nutritional composition of potatoes:

1. Carbohydrates: The potatoes contain primarily carbohydrates, the most important of which are starch. This starch may provide you with a constant release of energy, which will keep you feeling satisfied.

2. Fiber: The potato is a good source of dietary fibre, in particular if you eat it with the skin. The fibre provides energy to the digestive tract, promotes satiety and supports good gut health.

3. Vitamins: In addition to vitamin C, vitamins B6, potassium and Folate, potatoes are filled with a variety of vitamins. Antioxidant vitamins C and B6 are needed for brain development and

function, which is why they act as an antioxidant to support the immune system. Folate plays an essential role in the growth and development of cells as potassium is a crucial factor for regulating blood pressure.

4. Minerals: You can find minerals such as potassium, magnesium and iron in potatoes. These minerals play an essential role in maintaining proper muscle function, bone health and oxygen supply to the body.

Debunking Potato Myths

Potatoes have often been unjustly blamed for weight gain and associated with unhealthy eating habits. But there are some common myths about potatoes that we need to dispel:

1. Potatoes Cause Weight Gain: The potatoes themselves do not have a direct effect on weight gain. The contribution to weight gain is generated by the use of preparation methods accompanied by high calorie toppings. Potatoes may be part of a varied diet, provided that they are cooked properly and consumed with moderation.

2. Potatoes are High in Fat: In fact, although potatoes contain very low fats, cooking methods and flavourings can have a significant effect on their Fat content. Choose tastier cooking methods like baking, boiling or steaming and add healthy food such as herbals, spices or a little bit of olive oil.

3. Potatoes Lack Nutritional Value: As we discussed in the past, potatoes are a nutritious food with high levels of essential vitamins, minerals and fiber. The combination of potatoes and vegetables may provide a wellrounded meal that includes variety of vegetables and nutrient dense foods together with potatoes.

Embracing the Versatility of Potatoes

The potato is incredibly malleable and you can do a lot of wonderful things with it. Let's look at some of the possibilities for exploiting them.:

1. Baking and Roasting: A combination of herbs and spices can be used to cook or roast potatoes in a way that results in an aromatic, nutrientous dish or even a main course.

2. Mashing and Pureeing: Mashed potatoes can provide comfort and satisfaction as part of a meal. Add some extra nutrients and flavour by mixing steamed vegetables such as cauliflower or carrots.

3. Boiling and Steaming: The potatoes retain their natural flavours and nutrients when boiled or steamed. You can enjoy them as part of the meal, or you can add them to salads, soups and stews.

4. Exploring International Cuisine: In cuisine all over the world, potatoes are celebrated. Try a taste of potato recipes all over the world, such as Spanish tortilla and India's aloo gobi or Ireland's colcannon.

In this chapter, we've uncovered the potato phenomenon by delving into the historical significance of potatoes, their nutritional composition, and debunking common myths surrounding their consumption. Potatoes are a versatile, nutrient-dense food that can be enjoyed as part of a healthy diet. The potato's versatility can be harnessed and put to good use in a variety of foods for an entertaining and satisfying experience, when we understand its inherent potential and prepare it properly. Practical guidelines to select, store and prepare potatoes so as to maximise the benefits of them will be addressed within the next chapter. In your culinary adventures, prepare yourself for an unprecedented burst of potatoes' potential!

Chapter 3

The Science of Weight Management

We'll explore the science of weight management in this chapter, examining how body weight is influenced by these factors and strategies to achieve and maintain good health. You will be able to gain a deeper understanding of the science underpinning weight management, and how potatoes can play an essential role in balanced and sustainable approaches to maintaining healthy bodyweight by the end of this chapter. So we're going to explore fascinating science of weight management together!

The Basics of Weight Management

Weight management is a complex process influenced by various factors, including genetics, metabolism, lifestyle, and dietary choices. It involves achieving a balance between energy intake (calories consumed) and energy expenditure (calories burned). Instead of fast fixes or strict diets, sustainable eating habits and long term lifestyle changes are essential for effective weight management.

Energy Balance and Caloric Needs

The concept of energy balance plays an essential role in the management of weight. This means that the calories which are consumed through food and beverages, as well as those used in physical activity and basic bodily functions need to be balanced.

1. Caloric Intake: Individual factors such as age, gender, height, body weight and activity level play a role in the number of calories consumed. The size of portions and quality of foods eaten need to be taken into account.

2. Caloric Expenditure: Energy expenditure comprises three elements: basal metabolic rateBMR, physical activity and the nutritional effect of food. BMR is a measure of the calories consumed at rest to sustain essential bodily

functions, while activity as well as the effects of food on hormone levels are contributing to further calorie expenditure.

Factors Affecting Weight Management

Weight management is influenced by several factors that may influence a person's ability to control his or her weight and keep it under control. Let's take a look at these factors:

1. Genetics: In certain body types, genetic factors could predispose individuals to these bodies and influence their metabolism and fat stores. However, genetics do not determine a person's destiny, and lifestyle choices can still have a significant impact on weight management.

2. Metabolism: Metabolism is the process of converting food into energy by chemical processes in the body. Metabolism may be influenced by a range of factors, including age, body composition and exercise level, even though metabolism varies from person to person.

3. Lifestyle Factors: As regards weight management, the choice of lifestyle plays an important role. Overall well being and weight control are helped by a balanced level of physical activity, appropriate sleep, stress management as well as good dietary habits such as mindful eating.

The Role of Potatoes in Weight Management

With regard to the impact on weight management, potatoes are often subject to unwarranted criticism. However, potatoes may be beneficial in complementing a weight management plan if they are eaten as part of a balanced diet. Here's why:

1. Nutrient Density: While potatoes have relatively few calories, they are a vital source of nutrients such as vitamins, minerals and fiber. With no excessive intake of calories, they could contribute to a satisfying meal.

2. Satiety and Portion Control: There is a high satiety index in potatoes which helps to make you feel full and satisfied after eating. It may

help control the amount of food consumed and prevent eating too much.

3. Resistant Starch Content: As discussed in previous chapters, some varieties of potatoes have a starch resistance which makes it difficult to digest and can give you the taste of fullness while also promoting good digestion. For the purpose of weight control, this may be helpful.

4. Preparation Methods: The way potatoes are cooked may have a major influence on the amount of calories. Opting for healthier cooking methods like baking, boiling, or steaming, and avoiding excessive amounts of high-calorie toppings can make potatoes a nutritious and weight-friendly choice.

Strategies for Healthy Weight Management

To achieve and maintain a healthy weight, it's important to adopt sustainable strategies that focus on overall well-being. Here are some helpful strategies:

1. Balanced Diet: Make sure you're eating a balanced diet, in which vegetables, fruits, whole

grains, low protein and good fats are included. Establish potatoes as part of a balanced diet, focusing on portion control.

2. Mindful Eating: Practice mindful eating by paying attention to hunger and fullness cues, eating slowly, and savoring each bite. This can also help you avoid overeating and promote a good relationship with food.

3. Regular Physical Activity: You should be active regularly in activities which you enjoy, like walking, cycling, swimming or dancing. To support overall healthy and weight management, focus is placed on a combination of cardio exercise, strength training or flexibility exercises.

4. Behavior Modification: Focuses on the application of behavioural modification techniques, including setting achievable targets, tracking progress, coping with stress and trying to get help from friends, family or professionals if necessary.

In this chapter, we've explored the science behind weight management and how various factors influence body weight. We've also debunked the myths surrounding potatoes and their role in weight gain. Achieving and maintaining a healthy weight can be achieved when you are aware of the concept of energy balance, taking into account each individual factor as well as developing a holistic approach toweight management. When cooked correctly and eaten in a balanced diet, potatoes can add value to the food you eat. In the next chapter, we will focus on practical tips for incorporating potatoes into your everyday meals, providing you with delicious and nutritious recipe ideas. Get ready to elevate your culinary experience with the power of potatoes!

Chapter 4

Cultivating a Healthy Gut Microbiome

In this chapter, we will explore the fascinating world of the gut microbiome and its impact on overall health. We're going to look at the importance of building a healthy gut microbiome, as well as how consumption of resistant starchrich foods like potatoes can contribute to their good health. So, let us embark on a journey to discover the wonders of gut microbiome and learn how to nurture them for optimum health!

The Gut Microbiome: A Microscopic Ecosystem

The trillions of microorganism residing in our gastrointestinal tract are referred to as the gut microbiome. These organisms comprise a complex ecosystem that plays an important role in keeping us healthy, including bacteria, fungi, viruses and certain types of microbes.

1. Gut Microbiota: The term "gut microbiota" refers to the actual microorganisms residing in the gut, while the "gut microbiome" encompasses both the microorganisms and their genetic material.

2. Microbial Diversity: A healthy gut microbiome is characterized by a diverse array of microorganisms. Having a wide range of beneficial bacteria helps support various functions and promotes overall well-being.

The Role of the Gut Microbiome

The bacteria on our gut play an important role in many areas of health, including digestion, immunomodulatory function, metabolisms and the like. In this way, we'll look at its major roles:

1. Digestion and Nutrient Absorption: The microbial community in the gut is beneficial for breaking down and absorbing nutrients, e.g.

carbohydrates, fats or proteins. It produces enzymes to help digestion as well.

2. Immune System Support: A vital role in developing and functioning the immune system is played by an optimum Gut Microbiome. It assists in the control of immunological responses, protects against undesirable pathogens and promotes a balanced immunity system.

3. Metabolic Health: Recent research has shown that gut microbes, including weight management, sensitivity to insulin and regulation of sugar levels in the blood, are associated with metabolic health.

4. Mental Health and Brain Function: The gut-brain axis is a bidirectional communication pathway between the gut and the brain. Through this axis, the microbiome of the gut plays a role in brain function, mood and mental health.

Nurturing a Healthy Gut Microbiome

Let's look at strategies for growing and maintaining the well being of the microbiome, now that we understand the importance of good gut health:

1. Consuming Resistant Starch: Resistant starch acts like a prebiotic, which provides nutrients to beneficial bacteria in the gut. The potato provides a good source of resistant starch and may be beneficial for the health of your gut microflora, especially during cooking and cooling.

2. Including Fiber-Rich Foods: In order to grow and maintain the diversity of microbiomes in your gut, fibre is essential. In your diet include a selection of foods that are rich in fiber, for example whole grains, legumes, fruits and vegetables.

3. Probiotic and Fermented Foods: Probiotics are live beneficial bacteria that can be consumed through foods like yogurt, kefir, sauerkraut, and kimchi. The beneficial bacteria in the gut can be introduced into these foods, which are supportive of microbial diversity.

4. Minimizing Antibiotic Use: By indiscriminately killing harmful and beneficial

bacterial populations, antibiotics can disrupt the microbial community in the gut. Antibiotics should be used with caution and, if necessary, consideration should be given to supplementing the gut with probiotics to support the health of the gut during antibiotic therapy.

5. Managing Stress: The microbiome of the gut can be negatively affected by prolonged stress. In order to promote the good environment in your gut, you should adopt stress management techniques like meditation, exercise, better sleep and fun activities that you enjoy.

The Gut Microbiome and Resistant Starch in Potatoes

Potatoes are a delicious source of resistant starch, which is used as fuel for beneficial bacteria in the human digestive tract, particularly during cooking and cooling. It may contribute to a thriving microbial community in the gut when potatoes are incorporated into your diet. Here's how:

1. Cooling Potatoes: The potatoes are subjected to the retrogradation procedure, which allows

some of the starch to be resistant to digestion after cooking and cooling. It is increasing the content of resistant starch and providing nourishment for beneficial bacteria in the gut.

2. Balanced Preparation Methods: In order to preserve the favourable properties of potatoes, choose a healthier cooking method such as baking, boiling or steam rather than deepfrying. You can enjoy them with your skin because it contains additional fibre and nutrients.

3. Pairing with Fiber-Rich Foods: For the purpose of making a meal that supports various gut microbiome populations and contributes to healthy digestive health, combine your potato with other fiberrich foods such as vegetables, legumes or whole grains.

In this chapter, we've explored the captivating world of the gut microbiome and its significant impact on our health. Cultivating a healthy gut microbiome is crucial for digestion, immune function, metabolism, and mental well-being. We can feed beneficial intestinal bacteria and promote microbial diversity by eating resistant starch rich foods such as potatoes. The flourishing environment for the gut may also be enhanced through implementing strategies, like including fibrerich foods, probiotics and stress management. In the next chapter, We'll provide you with a good selection of delicious and nutritious recipes for potatoes that can be incorporated into your daily meals so as to enhance the benefits of resistant starch. Come on, let's get excited about the lovely taste and health benefits of potatoes!

Chapter 5

The Potato Hack Protocol

In this chapter, we will explore the concept of the Potato Hack Protocol, a strategy that utilizes potatoes as a primary food source for a designated period. In this session we'll look at the principles, benefits and practical implementation of Potato Hack Protocol which will provide you with a comprehensive understanding of our unique approach to exploiting the potentials of potatoes for health and wellbeing. We'll be diving into a world of potato hack protocol, shall we?

Understanding the Potato Hack Protocol

The Potato Hack Protocol is the temporary shift of dietary focus on potatoes in a particular time period. The aim of the experiment has been to make an immediate impact on changing dietary habits, promoting weight loss, improving insulin sensitivity and exploiting the therapeutic properties of resistant starch in potatoes. Let's take a look at the principles underpinning the Potato Hack Protocol:

1. Caloric Restriction: For the purpose of creating an insufficient number of calories and promoting weight loss, the potato hack protocol is typically to consume a limited amount of calories, in particular from potatoes.

2. Resistant Starch Intake: Resistance starch, which acts as an prebiotic and aids digestive health, is contained mainly in potatoes when they are cooked or cooled. During the given time, the Potato Hack Protocol ensures that resistant starch intake is maximized.

Benefits of the Potato Hack Protocol

When the Potato Hack Protocol is carried out correctly and in a reasonable period of time, it provides several possible benefits. We're going to talk about some of these advantages:

1. Weight Loss: The potato hack protocol is intended to reduce caloric intake, which can

result in weight loss if properly maintained. It may help to create a feeling of fullness and support portion moderation by having potatoes that have relatively low calories and high fibre content.

2. Insulin Sensitivity: Insulin sensitivity has been found to be enhanced due to the increased resistant starch content in potatoes. Individuals can experience better control of blood glucose and increased insulin responsiveness when potatoes are incorporated into their diet as part of the Potato Hack protocol.

3. Gut Health: In potatoes, resistant starch acts as a prebiotic, nourishing source of beneficial gut bacteria and supports a healthy gut microbiome. In a defined period the potato hack protocol can contribute to optimising gut health.

4. Food Relationship Reset: Individuals could benefit from a temporary shift to simple and limited foods, such as potatoes, for the purpose of recovering their relationship with food, supporting good dietary habits or preventing unhealthy eating patterns.

Implementing the Potato Hack Protocol

In order to ensure the appropriate level of compliance with your particular dietary needs and objectives, it is recommended that you have a consultation with healthcare professionals or certified nutritionists prior to starting this Potato Hack Protocol. To implement the Protocol on Potato Hack, here are some practical considerations:

1. Duration: A brief period of implementation, ranging from a few days to weeks, is usually required for the potato hack protocol. The specific duration should be defined according to individual objectives and in consultation with a healthcare professional.

2. Potato Variety and Preparation: Choose the variety of potatoes you enjoy, and it's in line with your diet. To bring variety to your meals, mix up the dishes by adding various cooking techniques such as boiling, steaming orbaking.

3. Meal Planning: During the Potato Hack protocol, it is necessary to plan your meals in advance so you are aware of what nutrition will

be required. Take a variety of potato dishes, which are packed with other vegetables, herbs and spices in order to provide flavour and added nutrients.

4. Hydration and Supplementation: Eat a good dose of water in the Potato Hack Protocol so that you are properly hydrated. If any additional supplements are needed to fulfil your dietary requirements, it may be useful to discuss this with a healthcare professional.

Transitioning and Long-Term Strategies

It is essential to return to a balance and sustainable eating pattern as soon as the designated period for implementation of the Potato Hack Protocol has expired. Here are some strategies to transition and take into account the lessons learnt from the potato hack protocol for long term habits:

1. Gradual Transition: In the short run, a more diverse variety of foods is gradually introduced while continuing to prioritise options with high levels of nutrients. To keep pace with your

energy needs and goals, you'll start to consume more calories in a gradual manner.

2. Mindful Eating and Portion Control: Continue to practice mindful eating and portion control, which you've learned from the potato hack protocol. Pay attention to hunger and fullness cues, savor each bite, and prioritize balanced meals.

3. Balanced Diet: Ensure that your diet consists of a wide range of whole foods, such as vegetables, fruits, proteins, healthy fats and grains. Potatoes, however, can still be part of your regular meals but they're more moderate and complement a well balanced diet.

In this chapter, we looked at the idea of a potato hack protocol for weight loss, improved insulin sensitivity and health in the gut, which is short term approach to exploit the nutritional benefits of potatoes. Individuals may benefit from a short period of time to concentrate on the consumption of potatoes and maximise their intake of resilient starch. However, in order to take the Potato Hack Protocol and move on to a balanced and sustainable diet afterwards, it is necessary to make use of guidance from healthcare professionals. In the next section, we'll be putting together a collection of great potato recipes that will satisfy your appetites while providing you with different options to make potatoes part of each day's well balanced diet. Get ready to savor the flavors and health benefits of these potato-inspired dishes!

Chapter 6

Recipes and Meal Plans

We're going to be giving you a collection of tasty and nutritious potato recipes and meal plans in this chapter. In addition to supporting your health and well being, these recipes will help you incorporate the goodness of potatoes into your daily meals. Get ready to embark on a culinary adventure with the versatile and nutritious potato!

Breakfast Recipes

- Potato and Vegetable Frittata

Ingredients:
- 2 medium potatoes, thinly sliced
- 1 cup mixed vegetables (such as bell peppers, onions, and spinach)
- 6 eggs
- ¼ cup milk
- Salt and pepper to taste
- Fresh herbs for garnish (optional)

Instructions:

1. Preheat the oven to 350°F (175°C). Place the sliced potatoes on a baking sheet and bake for 10-15 minutes until slightly tender.

2. In a skillet, sauté the mixed vegetables until they are cooked but still slightly crisp.

3. In a bowl, whisk together the eggs, milk, salt, and pepper.

4. Grease a baking dish and layer the partially cooked potatoes at the bottom. Top with the sautéed vegetables.

5. In order to make sure that the vegetables are uniformly mixed, spread the egg mixture over them.

6. Bake in the preheated oven for 20-25 minutes or until the frittata is set and slightly golden.

7. Garnish with fresh herbs if desired. Serve warm.

- Sweet Potato Pancakes

Ingredients:
- 2 cups cooked and mashed sweet potatoes
- 2 eggs
- ½ cup flour (can use whole wheat or gluten-free flour)

- 1 teaspoon baking powder
- ½ teaspoon cinnamon
- ¼ teaspoon nutmeg
- Pinch of salt
- Maple syrup and fresh fruits for serving

Instructions:
1. In a mixing bowl, combine the mashed sweet potatoes and eggs until well blended.
2. In a separate bowl, whisk together the flour, baking powder, cinnamon, nutmeg, and salt.
3. Slowly add the dry ingredient to the mixture of Sweet Potatoes, stirring constantly until it is all mixed together.
4. Heat a nonstick skillet or griddle over medium heat and lightly coat with cooking spray or oil.
5. Spoon the pancake batter onto the skillet, using about ¼ cup for each pancake. Cook until bubbles form on the surface, then flip and cook for an additional 1-2 minutes.
6. Maple syrup and fresh fruit are served with warm sweet potato pancakes.

Lunch and Dinner Recipes

- Baked Potato with Greek Salad

Ingredients:
- 2 large baking potatoes
- 1 cup cherry tomatoes, halved
- 1 cucumber, diced
- ½ red onion, thinly sliced
- ¼ cup Kalamata olives, pitted and sliced
- ½ cup crumbled feta cheese
- 2 tablespoons extra-virgin olive oil
- 1 tablespoon red wine vinegar
- Salt and pepper to taste
- Fresh parsley for garnish

Instructions:
1. Preheat the oven to 400°F (200°C). Wash and scrub the baking potatoes, then pierce them several times with a fork.
2. Place the potatoes directly on the oven rack and bake for 45-60 minutes, or until tender.
3. Put all the tomatoes, cucumbers, peppers, white onion, Kalama olives, feta cheese, olive oil, wine vinegar, salt and pepper into a bowl. Toss to combine.
4. Once the potatoes are cooked, cut a slit lengthwise in the top and gently squeeze the ends to open up the potato.

5. Add a mixture of Greek salad to the baked potatoes. Garnish with fresh parsley, and serve.

- Potato and Lentil Curry

Ingredients:
- 2 tablespoons coconut oil
- 1 onion, diced
- 2 garlic cloves, minced
- 1 tablespoon grated ginger
- 2 teaspoons curry powder
- 1 teaspoon ground cumin
- ½ teaspoon ground turmeric
- 2 cups diced potatoes
- 1 cup red lentils
- 4 cups vegetable broth
- 1 cup coconut milk
- Salt and pepper to taste
- Fresh cilantro for garnish

Instructions:
1. In a large pot, cook the coconut oil at moderate temperatures. Put a chopped onion, garlic and ginger in it. Sauté in the onion until it's transparent.
2. In the pot, mix the curry powder, cumin or turmeric for 1 minute to toast your spices.

3. Add the diced potatoes, lentils, vegetable broth, and coconut milk to the pot. Bring to a boil, then reduce the heat to low and simmer for 20-25 minutes, or until the lentils and potatoes are tender.

4. Season with salt and pepper to taste. If you want the curry to be more uniformly mixed, use a potato masher or immersion blender.

5. You'll be serving a warm potato and lentil curry, garnished with freshly pressed cilantro. Enjoy with steamed rice or naan bread.

Meal Planning Tips

You can make a healthy, balanced meal plan by incorporating potatoes which will help you to experience different kinds of nutrient and enjoyable meals during the week. Some good tips on how to properly plan meals are given below:

1. Plan Ahead: Planning your meals has to take a little bit of time every week, taking account of the timetable, nutrition preferences and nutritional needs. You'll be better organized and able to make more healthy choices.

2. Variety is Key: Mix together a variety of potato recipes, which mix up different cooking methods and flavours. It's going to make your meal exciting and you're going to get a lot of nutrients.

3. Balancing Macronutrients: In your potato based meals aim to include a balance between carbohydrates, proteins and healthy fats. In addition to vegetables and healthy fats such as avocado or olive oil, you can achieve this by taking in lean proteins like chicken breasts, fishmeatand legumes.

4. Portion Control: Keep an eye on portion sizes and take into account how hungry or full your body is. A balanced, satisfying meal may include a variety of colorful vegetables in addition to potatoes.

In this chapter, we have provided you with a selection of delicious and nutritious potato recipes and meal planning tips. From breakfast frittatas to lunch salads and hearty dinner curries, these recipes showcase the versatility and health benefits of potatoes. If you are planning to make a wide variety of meals, take into consideration adding other food groups like proteins, vegetables and good fats. You will enjoy the wonderful taste and nutritional benefits of potatoes, while enhancing your body's ability to absorb them, when you take a look at these recipes and incorporate them into your meal planning. In the next chapter, we will conclude our book and offer some final thoughts and tips for incorporating potatoes into a healthy lifestyle.

Chapter 7

Success Stories and Testimonials

In this chapter, we will share inspiring success stories and testimonials from individuals who have incorporated potatoes and the principles of resistant starch into their lives. Such stories are aimed at highlighting thetransformational strength of potatoes and how they have been positively linked to different aspects of health and well being. Prepare to be inspired by real life experiences and discover how potatoes have changed the lives of these individuals!

Story 1: Sarah's Weight Loss Journey

Sarah had struggled with her weight for years, trying countless diets and weight loss programs without sustainable results. She decided, however, to try it when she learned about the benefits of resistant starch and the Potato Hack Protocol. Sarah had been gradually and steadily losing weight as she concentrated on the addition of more potatoes to her meals. She felt better and avoided eating too much thanks to the large amounts of fiber in potatoes. Sarah's success illustrates the ability of potatoes to be a valuable tool in meeting weight reduction targets when accompanied by good food habits and healthy lifestyles.

Testimonial: "It never occurred to me that potatoes could be the key to my weight loss. I have been able to reset my food habits and learn the value of healthy meals thanks to the Potato Hack protocol. Now I've got a healthy relationship with food, and potatoes are the cornerstone of my diet. "I am very grateful for the impact they've made in terms of my weight loss and general well being."

Story 2: Mark's Improved Digestive Health

Mark had been struggling with digestive issues for years, experiencing bloating, irregular bowel movements, and discomfort after meals. He had made the decision to incorporate more potatoes into his diet after having learned about the advantages of resistance starch and its impact on gut health. When resistant starch in potato was used for the purpose of prebiotics and as a resource to promote gut bacteria, Mark remarked that his symptoms of digestion improved significantly. In addition, the added fiber content made his bowels easier to control. The use of potatoes for the promotion of good gut microbiomes and improvement in digestion is demonstrated by Mark's story.

Testimonial: "Potatoes have been instrumental in the improvement of my digestive system. I've been feeling bloated and uncomfortable for a long time, but after the potatoes were added to my meals, I saw an amazing improvement. My gut feels happier and more balanced, and I no longer dread mealtime. Potatoes have become my go-to food for promoting a healthy gut." - Mark

Story 3: Emily's Energy Boost

She had a low level of energy, and she was constantly tired. It was difficult to maintain focus and productivity throughout the day, she found. Emily decided to add more potatoes to her diet as soon as she learned the benefits of resistance starch and its role in stabilising blood sugar levels. An important increase in her energy level, as well as clarity of thought, was noted. She had a steady supply of energy all day long thanks to the slowly releasing carbohydrates in potato, which allowed her to feel more alert and efficient. Emily's story reminds us that potatoes can be an important source of energy, and are useful to fight fatigue.

Testimonial: "Potatoes have become my secret weapon for increasing energy levels. For most of my day, I have depended on sugar and caffeine for energy to keep me going, but since putting potatoes in my diet, I've felt an immediate and long lasting boost. I'm not experiencing energy blackouts anymore, and it gives me a greater sense of focus and productivity. "My everyday life has truly changed as a result of potatoes."

These stories of achievement and testimonials demonstrate the benefits that can be achieved by potatoes or resistant starch in people's lives. Potatoes have the potential of being an important addition to a good lifestyle, whether it's weight loss, improvement in digestion, increased energy or other benefits.

Remember, the journey of all people is unique and results may be different. A consultation with a healthcare professional or registered dietitian before you make major changes in your eating pattern remains the best advice. It will be able to provide you with personalised guidance and support based on your specific needs and health objectives.

In the next and final chapter of this book, we'll give you some ideas on how potatoes can be integrated into a long term healthy eating plan, as well as additional sources to explore further.

Conclusion

Congratulations! You've reached the final chapter of our book, "The Power of Potatoes: Unlocking the Health Benefits of Resistant Starch." In this journey, we've explored the incredible potential of potatoes to be a source of resistance starch and its effects on weight management, gut health, energy levels as well as wellbeing in general. In order to help you get the goodness of potatoes in your everyday life, we've provided you with all sorts of information, tips and tasty recipes. When we finish this book, let's look back at some of the major lessons learnt and give a few final thoughts on how to incorporate potatoes in our long term healthy lives eating plan.

Key Takeaways:

1. Resistant Starch: Resistant starch, a dietary fibre that resists digestion in the small intestine and is carried intact through the large intestine, is present in potatoes. There are numerous health benefits for this type of starch, e.g. an

improvement in insulin sensitivity, reduced bodyweight and better gut health.

2. Weight Management: In order to lose weight, the Potato Hack Protocol, a short term approach to maximising the intake of resistant starch, may be effective. Individuals can benefit from satisfying food, while being encouraged to lose weight and create healthy eating habits by concentrating on potato intake and learning the principles of mindful eating.

3. Gut Health: Resistant starch has been shown to be a prebiotic, feeding beneficial bacteria into your gut and supporting the healthy gastrointestinal microbiome. To improve digestive function, increase nutrient absorption and strengthen the health of the entire gut, it is possible to incorporate resistance starchrich foods such as potatoes.

4. Energy Boost: Slow release carbohydrates in the potato provide a steady source of energy and are able to fight fatigue. You'll be able to reap the benefits of a higher energy level, clearer thinking and better performance every day when potatoes are added to your meals.

5. Long-Term Approach: However, it is important to transition back into a balanced and sustainable eating pattern as the Potato Hack protocol offers short term benefits. Slowly, we're going to restore more variety of food, look for nutrient density options and continuing our practice of nutrition awareness and portion control.

Incorporating Potatoes into a Healthy Eating Plan

1. Variety and Balance: Try to get a variety of potatoes such as sweet potatoes, white potatoes, purple and fingerling potatoes. Each variety has a distinct taste and nutrition profile. In order to produce balanced meals, they should be complemented by a wide variety of vegetables, proteins and healthy fats.

2. Cooking Methods: In order to enjoy the flexibility of a potato, experiment with different cooking methods. Try to bake, roast, steam or mash them. There are a variety of textures and flavors in each method.

3. Recipes and Meal Planning: In planning your meals, incorporate the recipes for potatoes set out in Chapter 6. These recipes offer a range of options for keeping the meal interesting and healthy, such as breakfast frittatas to lunch salads or dinner curries.

4. Mindful Eating: Practice to eat well by savoring each bite, slowing down and taking into account your body's hunger and satiety signals. This approach will help you improve your healthy relationships with food and promote good health in general.

5. Professional Guidance: You should consult with a healthcare professional or registered dietitian before making any significant changes to your diet. Based on your specific needs and health goals they may be able to give you personalised advice and support.

Final Thoughts

In a number of cultures potatoes have traditionally been the traditional food source, and its advantages are much greater than just nutrition. You can unlock their full potential to improve your health and well being by using the power of resistant starch and incorporating potatoes into a balanced and mindful eating plan. You know, there's no such thing as a one size fits all approach. Listen to your body and make decisions that work best for you.

Hopefully, this book will inspire you to think about the health advantages of potatoes and how they can enhance your meals with great nutrition. You can enjoy potato's taste, while boosting your body with the necessary nutrients and promoting optimum health if you add potatoes in your day to day life.

We'd like to thank you for joining us in this potato filled journey, and we wish you the best of luck as you embark on your way towards a more healthy and happier life.

Happy Potato Adventures Ahead!

About the Author

Tony Steele is a passionate advocate for health and wellness, specializing in the transformative power of nutrition. With years of experience in the field, Tony has dedicated himself to exploring the potential of natural foods and their impact on our well-being. He is the author of "The Power of Potatoes: Unlocking the Health Benefits of Resistant Starch" where he shares his knowledge and insights.

Tony's personal health journey led him to discover the remarkable benefits of incorporating potatoes into a balanced diet, with their resistant starch content. The writer's style is friendly, easy to read, and makes the complicated science concepts available to a wide range of readers. In order to create a compelling and informative reading experience, Tony blends scientific evidence with practical advice and personal stories.

Throughout the book, Tony includes real-life success stories, showcasing the transformative effects that potatoes and resistant starch can have on individuals' lives. He believes in the power of these stories to inspire and motivate readers.

In addition to his passion for potatoes, Tony advocates an overall approach of health and wellbeing which stresses the importance of nutrition, physical activity, rest, mental well being. The author suggests that readers be encouraged to practice a balanced lifestyle, which is good for their health and vitality.

Join Tony Steele in "The Power of Potatoes: Unlocking the Health Benefits of Resistant Starch" as he shares his knowledge, experiences, and insights to empower readers on their own journey towards optimal health and well-being.

Printed in Great Britain
by Amazon